IT'S TIME TO EAT BLOOD ORANGES

It's Time to Eat BLOOD ORANGES

Walter the Educator

Silent King Books
A WhichHead Entertainment Imprint

Copyright © 2024 by Walter the Educator

All rights reserved. No part of this book may be reproduced in any manner whatsoever without written per- mission except in the case of brief quotations embodied in critical articles and reviews.

First Printing, 2024

Disclaimer

This book is a literary work; the story is not about specific persons, locations, situations, and/or circumstances unless mentioned in a historical context. Any resemblance to real persons, locations, situations, and/or circumstances is coincidental. This book is for entertainment and informational purposes only. The author and publisher offer this information without warranties expressed or implied. No matter the grounds, neither the author nor the publisher will be accountable for any losses, injuries, or other damages caused by the reader's use of this book. The use of this book acknowledges an understanding and acceptance of this disclaimer.

It's Time to Eat BLOOD ORANGES is a collectible early learning book by Walter the Educator suitable for all ages belonging to Walter the Educator's Time to Eat Book Series. Collect more books at WaltertheEducator.com

USE THE EXTRA SPACE TO TAKE NOTES AND DOCUMENT YOUR MEMORIES

BLOOD ORANGES

The winter breeze is crisp and cold,

It's Time to Eat
Blood
Oranges

But here's a secret to be told:

A fruit that's juicy, sweet, and bright,

Blood oranges are such a delight!

Peel the skin, so thick and fine,

And see the color, deep as wine.

A ruby glow, a dazzling hue,

Inside, a treasure waits for you!

Take a bite, it's tart and sweet,

A burst of sunshine, a special treat.

It tastes like berries, citrus, and more,

A flavor mix you'll just adore.

"Why are they red?" you might ask me,

"It's like a sunset in a tree!"

The color comes from sunshine's touch,

A gift from nature, thanks so much!

It's Time to Eat Blood Oranges

Slice them thin or eat them whole,

Blood oranges warm the heart and soul.

In salads, drinks, or on a plate,

Every way, they taste just great!

The juice is crimson, rich, and bright,

Perfect for sipping morning or night.

Squeeze it fresh, let it flow,

A cup of magic, watch it glow!

"Mommy, look!" I shout with cheer,

"The best fruit's finally here!"

She smiles and says, "Let's share this treat,

Blood oranges make life so sweet."

Friends gather 'round, we share a bite,

Smiles grow big, eyes shine with light.

The taste of winter, bold and fun,

It's Time to Eat Blood Oranges

Blood oranges for everyone!

The season's short, they won't stay long,

So let's enjoy them while they're strong.

A fruit so rare, a gift so true,

Blood oranges are made for you!

Peel, slice, sip, or make a pie,

Blood oranges make spirits fly.

So when it's time, don't wait or stall,

It's Time to Eat
Blood Oranges

Hooray for blood oranges, loved by all!

ABOUT THE CREATOR

Walter the Educator is one of the pseudonyms for Walter Anderson. Formally educated in Chemistry, Business, and Education, he is an educator, an author, a diverse entrepreneur, and he is the son of a disabled war veteran. "Walter the Educator" shares his time between educating and creating. He holds interests and owns several creative projects that entertain, enlighten, enhance, and educate, hoping to inspire and motivate you. Follow, find new works, and stay up to date with Walter the Educator™

at WaltertheEducator.com

www.ingramcontent.com/pod-product-compliance
Lightning Source LLC
LaVergne TN
LVHW052010060526
838201LV00059B/3961